ELVIS COSTELLO

SPIKE

D1471472

WISE PUBLICATIONS
LONDON/NEW YORK/SYDNEY

EXCLUSIVE DISTRIBUTORS:
MUSIC SALES LIMITED
8/9 FRITH STREET,
LONDON W1V 5TZ.
ENGLAND.

MUSIC SALES PTY LIMITED
120 ROTHSCHILD AVENUE,
ROSEBERY, NSW 2018,
AUSTRALIA.

THIS BOOK © COPYRIGHT 1989 BY
WISE PUBLICATIONS

UK ISBN 0.7119.1843.0.
ORDER NO. AM74923

ARRANGED BY ROGER DAY
MUSIC PROCESSED BY BARNES MUSIC ENGRAVING
TYPESET BY TEXT UNIT

MUSIC SALES' COMPLETE CATALOGUE LISTS THOUSANDS OF TITLES AND IS FREE FROM YOUR LOCAL MUSIC SHOP,
OR DIRECT FROM MUSIC SALES LIMITED. PLEASE SEND £1 IN STAMPS FOR POSTAGE TO
MUSIC SALES LIMITED, 8/9 FRITH STREET, LONDON W1V 5TZ.

PRINTED IN THE UNITED KINGDOM BY
THE CAMELOT PRESS LIMITED, SOUTHAMPTON, HAMPSHIRE.

...THIS TOWN...
WORDS & MUSIC BY D.P.A. MAC MANUS

Verses 1 and 2

That Char-lie Se-dar - ka was a-play-ing the pia - no, like he was paw-ing a dir - ty book.

He bit a hole_ in his big___ bot-tom lip_ and gave his ver - y best lit - tle boy look.___

It was a song with a to-pic-al verse which I'm a - fraid he then pro-ceed-ed to sing,___ some-thing a - bout the mood - y doomed love of a

fish fin - ger (beau - ty is there___ in my) king. You're

no - bo - dy in this town, You're no - bo - dy in

this crowd, You're no - bo - dy till ev - ery - bo - dy in

this town, thinks you're pois - on, got your num - ber, knows it

5

girl with the e-ter-ni-ty rock___ went down on her book-ie to buy some stock.___ Now all the

signs in the shop-ping ar-cades___ say 'The corp-or-a-tion thief is the new___ Jes-se James.'(2.) Her
(3.) They made

(fet-ish of the hour.) You're

You're no-bo-dy in this town, you're

Verse 2
Mr Getgood moved up to Self-made Man Row
Although he swears that he's the salt of the earth.
He's so proud of the 'kick-me-hard' sign
that they hung on his back at birth.
He said, 'I appreciate beauty, if I have one, then it's my fault.'
'Beauty is on my pillow, beauty is there in my vault.'

Verse 3
(Part 2)
Her clothes and her attention were scant, her eyes were everywhere,
Her eyes were like absinthe.
The little green figures that dance on his screen say everything you
want to hear and nothing they mean.
(Part 3)
They made love while she was changing her dress.
She wiped him off, she wiped him out and then she made him confess.
A little amused by the belief in her power
You must remember this was the fetish of the hour.

LET HIM DANGLE

WORDS & MUSIC BY D.P.A. MAC MANUS

Let him dan - gle,_____ Do do do do do do do do do.

4th time continue

D.C.
to fade on chorus (ad lib)

From a

Verse 2
Bentley had surrendered, he was under arrest
When he gave Chris Craig that fatal request
Craig shot Sidney Miles, he took Bentley's word
The prosecution claimed as they charged him with murder . . .

Verse 3
They said Derek Bentley was easily led
Well what's that to the woman that Sidney Miles wed
Though guilty was the verdict and Craig had shot him dead
The gallows were for Bentley and still she never said . . .

Verse 4
Not many people thought that Bentley would hang
But the word never came, the phone never rang
Outside Wandsworth Prison there was horror and hate
As the hangman shook Bentley's hand to calculate his weight . . .

Verse 5
From a welfare state to society murder
'Bring back the noose' is always heard
Whenever those swine are under attack
But it won't make you even, it won't bring him back . . .

DEEP DARK TRUTHFUL MIRROR

WORDS & MUSIC BY D.P.A. MAC MANUS

One day you're going to have to face a deep dark truth-ful mir -

- ror and its going to tell you things that I still

love you too much to say.

1st time only

2nd and 3rd time

(some - where well you)

The sky was just a pur - ple bruise, the ground was ir -

deep dark truth-ful___ mir-ror.   (2.) Now the

mir-ror.   So you bay for the boy in the tig-er-skin trunks,   they set him up,

set him up on the stool.   He falls__ down, he falls___ down like a drunk,___

and you drink till you drool,   and it's his sto-ry you'll

Verse 2
Now the flagstone streets where the newspaper shouts
ring to the boots of roustabouts
But you're never in any doubt, there's something happening somewhere.
Well you chase down the road till your fingers bleed
On a fibreglass tumbleweed
You can blow around the town, but it all shuts down the same.

Verse 3
A stripping puppet on a liquid stick gets into it pretty thick.
A butterfly drinks a turtle's tears,
but how do you know he really needs it?
'Cos a butterfly feeds on a dead monkey's hand;
Jesus wept, He felt abandoned.
You're a spellbound baby there's no doubting that.
Did you ever see a stare like a Persian cat?

VERONICA
WORDS & MUSIC BY D.P.A. MAC MANUS & PAUL McCARTNEY

-ro-ni-ca, Ve - ro-ni-ca.

to Coda

(2.) Did the
(3.) Ve -

2.
Half tempo

On the 'Em-press of In - di - a'_____ and as she closed her eyes up-on the

world and picked up-on the bones of last week's news,___ she spoke his name out loud a-gain.___

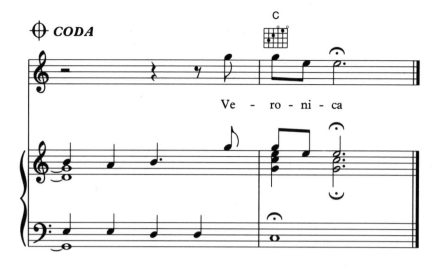

Verse 2

Did the days drag by? Did the favours wane?
Did he roam down the town all the time?
Will you wake from your dream with a wolf at the door,
Reaching out for Veronica?
Well it was all of sixty-five years ago
When the world was the street where she lived,
And a young man sailed on a ship in the sea
With a picture of Veronica.

Verse 3

Veronica sits in her favourite chair
And she sits very quiet and still,
And they call her a name that they never get right
And if they don't then nobody else will.
But she used to have a carefree mind of her own,
With devilish look in her eye,
Saying, 'You can call me anything you like, but
My name is Veronica'.

GOD'S COMIC
WORDS & MUSIC BY D.P.A. MAC MANUS

I wish you'd known me when I was a-live,___ I was a fun-ny

fel - ler.___ The crowd would hoot and hol - ler for more,___

I wore a drunk's red nose for app - lause.___ (Re - qui - em)

my re-ward._ I was scared,_ I was scared, I was scared,_ I was scared,

He might have ne - ver heard God's___ com-ic.___

I'm going to take a lit - tle trip down pa - ra -

-di-se's end-less shores._ They say that tra-vel broad-ens the mind,_ till you can't get your

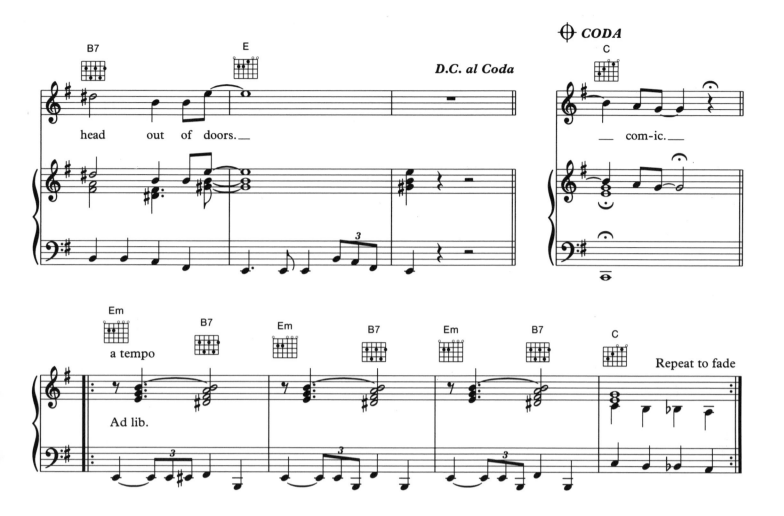

Verse 2
So there he was on a water-bed
Drinking a cola of a mystery brand
Reading an airport novelette,
Listening to Andrew Lloyd Webber's 'Requiem'
He said, before it had really begun,
'I prefer the one about my son.'
'I've been wading through all this unbelievable junk
And wondering if I should have given the world to the monkeys.'

Verse 3
I'm sitting here on the top of the world
I hang around in the longest night
Until each beast has gone to bed
And then I say 'God bless' and turn out the light.
While you lie in the dark, afraid to breathe
And you beg and you promise and you bargain and you plead.
Sometimes you confuse me with Santa Claus
It's the big white beard I suppose.
I'm going up the pole, where you folks die of cold.
I might be gone for a while if you need me.

Chorus 3rd time
Now I'm dead, Now I'm dead, Now I'm dead, Now I'm dead,
And you're all going on to meet your reward.
Are you scared? Are you scared? Are you scared? Are you scared?
You might never have heard, but God's comic.

CHEWING GUM
WORDS & MUSIC BY D.P.A. MAC MANUS

With their card-board hands by their sides, here's a nak-ed man and la-dy, and they're yours to cut out and keep,

so you can dress them up may-be.

They don't know just who they are or who they're sup-posed to be,___

you can make them hap-py or sad,___ or as-sume their i - den - ti - ty.___

1st time

1.

2.3.

There must be some-thing that is bet-ter than this.___ It starts with a slap_ and ends with a kiss,_

__ be-gins with you bawl - ing and it ends up in tears._____ Oh__ my lit - tle one,

take that chew-ing gum out of your ears.

Though he on - ly taught her three lit - tle words, it does-n't mat-ter if they're dir - ty or clean.

He can on-ly con-trol what they look_ like. He can ne - ver poss-ess__ what they mean.__

26

Verse 2
So here they are in the departure lounge.
It's the 'Gateway to the East.'
She is just another mail-order bride
She doesn't know he's a kinky beast.
So he gives her a picture of Maradona and child
she wants to 'roll and rock.'
As he spills his beer over her,
bumps and grinds, as he repeats 'Bang-Cock'

Verse 3
She might as well be in the jungle
She might as well be on the moon
He's away on a business trip,
in Düsseldorf but she's becoming immune
to the lack of glamour and danger
in a West German city today.
The nearest she comes to the 'Dynasty' he promised her
Is a Chinese take-away.

Dal Segno
So he wants to whisper in her ear
All the shrinking nothingness
But something always comes between them
I wonder if you can guess.

TRAMP THE DIRT DOWN

WORDS & MUSIC BY D.P.A. MAC MANUS

-li - ti - cal cam - paign. A wo - man was

kiss - ing a child who was ob - vi - ous -

-ly in pain. She spills with com - pass -

- ion as that young child's

face in her hand she grips. Can you im - a - gine all that greed and a - var - ice com - ing down on____ that child's__ lips? Well I hope I don't die too soon, I pray the Lord my

soul to save. Yes I'll be a good boy.

I'm try-ing so hard to be-have.

Be-cause there's one thing I know, I'd like to live

long e-nough to sa-vour. That's when

England was the whore of the world, Marga-ret was her mad-am,_____ and the fu-ture looked as bright and as clear as the black tar-mac-a-dam,_____ Well I hope that

she sleeps well at night,___ is-n't haun - ted by

G7 C Am

eve - ry tin - y de - tail, when she held that love - ly

Am/G♯ Am/G D

face in her hands, all she thought of was be -

Em

- tray - al.

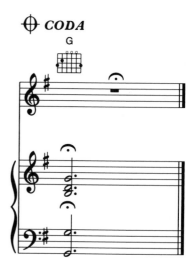

Verse 2
And now the cynical ones say that it all ends the same in the long run.
Try telling that to the desperate father who just squeezed the life
from his only son,
And how it's only voices in your head and dreams you never dreamt.
(Try telling him the subtle difference between justice and contempt.)

Verses at A
1. (Try telling me she isn't angry with this pitiful discontent.)
2. When they flaunt it in your face as you line up for punishment.
3. And then expect you to say 'Thank you', straighten up, look proud
   and pleased.
4. Because you've only got the symptoms, you haven't got the whole disease.
5. Just like a schoolboy, whose head's like a tin can, filled up with
   dreams then poured down the drain.
6. Try telling that to the boys on both sides, being blown to bits or
   beaten and maimed.

D.S.
Well I hope you live long now, I pray the Lord your soul to keep
I think I'll be going before we fold our arms and start to weep.
I never thought for a moment that human life could be so cheap
'Cause when they finally put you in the ground,
They'll stand there laughing and tramp the dirt down.

STALIN MALONE

WORDS & MUSIC BY D.P.A. MAC MANUS

SATELLITE
WORDS & MUSIC BY D.P.A. MAC MANUS

She's mad - ly ex - cit - ed now,

she throws her hands up like a tu - lip.

Not 1st time

Cue 2° (As he)
3° (in the hot)

She looks like an

il - lus - tra - tion of a cock - tail

par - ty, where car - toon bub - bles burst

in the air, champ - agne rolls off her

tongue____ like a sec - ond lang - uage.____

And it should have been her

shar - ing the same _____ sor - row. As the

sat - el - lite looks down, her

dark - est hour is some - bo - dy's bright to -

- mor - row.

man teth - er his _____ own bo - dy _____ to his dream, his dream to some - one else. _____ Oh no, oh no _____

time,   all   o - ver   the   world._____

The   sat - el - lite_____   looks   down_____   right

now_____   and   for - ev - er.   What

Verse 2
He pulled on a cigarette, in the crook of his first finger.
Felt the static electric charge of her perfect hour-glass figure
As he undressed her with his eyes her weakness was his talent.
How could she know as she stepped through the lights,
That her dress would become transparent.
And with his face pressed to the screen,
He muttered words he'd never dare to say if she could see him.
All over the world at the very same time
People sharing the same cheap sensation
The thrill of watching somebody watching those forbidden things
We never mention.

She went back to a pitiful compromise,
He'd go back to his family.
But for the matter of a thousand miles that separated them entirely.
In the hot loving spotlight, with secrets it arouses,
Now they both know what it's like inside a pornographer's trousers,
And in a funny way, it's anonymous, the satellite it blesses us,
And makes these dreams come true.

PADS, PAWS AND CLAWS

WORDS & MUSIC BY D.P.A. MAC MANUS & PAUL McCARTNEY

paws and claws.

2. And

She pads,____ pads____ a - round the bed - room,

pract - is - ing ways to flirt.____ He paws,____ pours_

__ a - no - ther drink and an - y - thing in____ a skirt,____

Verse 2

And if he should wake up in some terrible dive

And he don't know if he's so-so but he's so surprised he's alive

'Come on little honey, let me under your hive'

She pads paws, pads paws and claws.

Verse 3

She's got spider leg fingers, sharpened whenever he strays

And she carries a bird-purse with all of her womanly ways

While he's drinking hairspray, she knows that he would never dare

She could be in pictures if she wasn't all covered in fur.

BABY PLAYS AROUND

WORDS & MUSIC BY D.P.A. MAC MANUS & CAIT O'RIORDAN

1. It's not o-pen to dis-cus-sion an-y-more,
2. It's not o-pen to dis-cus-sion an-y-more,

She's out___ a-gain to-night, And I'm a-lone once more.
She walks_ these shi-ny streets, I walk the worn out floor.

She's all I have worth wait-ing for, but Ba-by plays a - round.
She's all I have worth liv-ing for,

And so it seems___ I've al-ways been the last to know,

MISS MACBETH

WORDS & MUSIC BY D.P.A. MAC MANUS

ceil-ing.___ Her blood-less face ran red in-side but was she real-ly ev-il, was she on-ly pan-to-mime?

A tempo

(1.) Now the chalk on the wall says that some-bo-dy saves, that some-bo-dy's face has just been washed off the pave-ment in-to a puz-zle where pet-rol will be pois-oned by rain. Miss Mac -

Some-times peo-ple are just____ what they app-ear to be with no re-demp-tion at all.___

___ We try to walk up-right when we can't ev - en___ crawl.___

D.%. al Coda

Miss Mac - - beth? Miss Mac -

- beth, Miss Mac - beth.

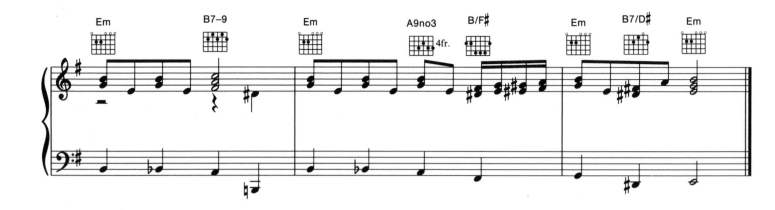

Verse 2
Well we all should have known when the children paraded.
They portrayed her in their fairy tales, sprinkling Deadly Nightshade,
And as they tormented her she rose to the bait,
Even a scapegoat must have someone to hate.

And every day she lives out another love song.
'You're up there enjoying yourself, and I know it's wrong'.
Well how can you miss what you've never possessed
Miss Macbeth, Miss Macbeth.

Verse 3
Miss Macbeth has a gollywog she chucks under the chin,
And she whispers to it tenderly, then sticks it on a pin
And it might be coincidence, but a boy down the lane,
That she said went as white as he could do, then doubled over in pain.

And every day she lives out . . . *etc. as 1st verse*

ANY KING'S SHILLING

WORDS & MUSIC BY D.P.A. MAC MANUS

(1.) You're a   fine one, oh   yes you are.   You're a
ans - wer   when they make that call.   Pull up -
know if   what I'm doing is right.   I don't

is - n't worth an - y king's shill - ing.___ I will

Please don't put your sil - ly head in that pret - ty sol - dier's
Please don't put your sil - ly head in that Brit - ish sol - dier's

hat, you've done your du - ty, that's e - nough of
hat, you've done your du - ty, that's e - nough of

3rd time segue

that. (2° v3) I don't fine one, oh yes you are, you're a fine one just like me.
that. (3°) You're a

COAL TRAIN ROBBERIES

WORDS & MUSIC BY D.P.A. MAC MANUS

Verse 2
While all the time in the camptown theatres of Piccadilly,
They're going to throw a black-face minstrel show
For the barefoot children that they're always selling.
They'll say, 'It's quaint', as the guilty ones faint
And claim they ain't underneath this paint.
We interrupt these liberal saints with their whips and watermelon.

Verse 3
So we return to the whitewashed pout of his committee lips,
Since he was declared the long lost fountain of youth
that drips and drips and drips.
1st time
They'll be sending him round from door to door,
to sell you back what's already yours.
2nd time
'So many good deeds, so little time'
Say the advertising agency swine.
3rd time
When man has destroyed what he thinks he owns,
I hope no living thing cries over his bones.
If you don't believe that I'm going for good,
You can count the days I'm gone and chop up the chairs for firewood.

LAST BOAT LEAVING
WORDS & MUSIC BY D.P.A. MAC MANUS

Hush my lit-tle one___ don't cry___ so, you know your Dad - dy's___ bound to go. They took his pride, they took his voice. Don't up - set him now, don't make a noise. They said, 'You're luck - y son,

you've still got a choice'. Last boat leav - ing. Don't

waste your tears, it's not as if___ I'm in chains. I don't want to go___ now,

it would be bet - ter for you___ too, if you don't look back___ when we

sail.___
(Last boat leav - ing, last boat leav - ing.) (Last boat leav - ing.) So

You've had my in-no-cence, you've had my heart - break, you've tak-en the place, where I once be-longed, now

what more can you take? _____

Verse 2
Hush my dear, while I whisper it in your ear,
We're not going to sail tonight, we're going to disappear
And it feels like a punishment, but I don't know what for.
Take care of your mother, son, it's you that she adores,
'Cos no matter how long we sail we'll never reach the shore.
Last boat leaving.

Don't waste your tears.
It's not as if I'm in chains.
When you go to school, son, you'll read my story in history books
Only they won't mention my name.